STONES, BONES, AND PETROGLYPHS

DIGGING INTO SOUTHWEST ARCHAEOLOGY

by SUSAN E. GOODMAN

photographs by MICHAEL J. DOOLITTLE

ALADDIN PAPERBACKS

AN ULTIMATE FIELD TRIP

First Aladdin Paperbacks edition September 2000
Previously published as *Stones, Bones, and Petroglyphs:*
Digging into Southwest Archaeology by Atheneum Books for Young Readers.

Text copyright © 1998 by Susan E. Goodman

Photographs copyright © 1998 by Michael J. Doolittle

ALADDIN PAPERBACKS
An imprint of Simon & Schuster Children's Publishing Division
1230 Avenue of the Americas
New York, NY 10020

Also available in an Atheneum Books for Young Readers hardcover edition

Book design by Anne Scatto/PIXEL PRESS

The text for this book was set in Monotype Fournier.

Printed and bound in Hong Kong

10 9 8 7 6 5 4 3 2 1

The Library of Congress has catalogued the hardcover edition as follows:
Goodman Susan E., 1952-
Stones, bones, and petroglyphs : digging into Southwest archaeology / by Susan E. Goodman;
photographs by Michael J. Doolittle.—1st ed.
p. cm.
Includes bibliographical references.
ISBN 0-689-81121-7
1. Pueblo Indians—Antiques—Juvenile literature. 2. Excavations (Archaeology)—Colorado—Mesa
Verde National Park—Juvenile literature. 3. Mesa Verde National Park (Colo.)—Antiquities—Juvenile
literature. I. Doolittle, Michael J. II. Title.
E99.P9G66 1998
978.8'27—dc21
97-6501
ISBN: 0-689-83891-3 (Aladdin pbk.)

Petroglyphs are pictures carved into rock. Some people believe this one tells the story of the ancient Pueblo migration.

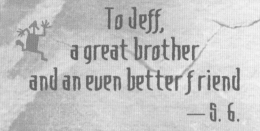

To Jeff,
a great brother
and an even better friend
— S. G.

To Don,
who is the only reason
I am a photographer
— M. D.

We'd like to thank the crew from Hannibal—the kids, Diane Kocher, Linda Mahlia, and especially Pat Mahlia—for inviting us along. Thanks to the entire staff at Crow Canyon, particularly Sara Kelly, Ken Lanik, Pam Wheat, Lew Matis, Chris Pierce, Bruce Bradley, Shannon Gallagher, and Ricky Lightfoot for his technical review. Susan Thomas allowed us to photograph at the Anasazi Heritage Center and Kathleen Brown of the Chamber of Commerce lined up the generous support of the Lebanon Schoolhouse Bed and Breakfast.

Thanks to Don Heiny for his help with picture editing, readers Deborah Hirschland and Majorie Waters for their invaluable input, Howard Kaplan for running interference, and Anne Scatto for yet another beautiful layout. And thanks to Marcia Marshall, who is always in our corner.

Contents

Chapter 1
A LONG TIME AGO . . .   6

Chapter 2
GOOPING UP AND SETTING OFF   8

Chapter 3
THE FACTS ABOUT ARTIFACTS   17

Chapter 4
DIGGING INTO THE PAST   24

Chapter 5
TRYING OUT THE OLD WAYS   32

Chapter 6
VISITING THE PAST   39

Glossary   46

Further Reading/More Information   48

A LONG TIME AGO . . .

After a hot day in his cornfield, the man drops his digging stick and slowly lowers himself over the canyon's edge. Clinging to the wall with his hands, he uses his foot to feel for the holes his people have pecked into the stone. Carefully, he inches down to the village built right into the cliff . . .

For over a thousand years, Pueblo people lived on mesas, or canyon tops, in a part of the American Southwest called the Four Corners, where Colorado, New Mexico, Utah, and Arizona meet. Suddenly, around A.D. 1200, these people moved into giant alcoves that nature had cut into the middle of canyon walls. They created their Stone Age apartment buildings by chipping out one stone block after another. To make the mud that held these blocks in place, they carried water up hundreds of feet from a spring on the canyon floor. All that work—and they used these buildings for just a few decades.

By the year 1300, every Pueblo man, woman, and child had left the Four Corners area.

These hand-and-toe-holds helped people climb steep cliffs.

Their fire pits held only ashes. Their fields fed only birds and animals. Their cities stood empty and silent.

We know where these people went. They moved south into what is now New Mexico and Arizona. But why did they leave the land they had lived in for more than one thousand years?

This is just one question archaeologists at Crow Canyon Archaeological Center in Colorado are trying to answer. Archaeologists study people of the past, and these archaeologists are working to understand who these Puebloans were and how they lived. They excavate, or dig, in ruins to help build a picture of this ancient world.

Now the archaeologists have help. A group of eighth-graders from Hannibal Middle School in Hannibal, Missouri, came to Crow Canyon to learn what these scientists already know.

And to help them find new answers.

The Hannibal kids and their advisers (left to right):

STANDING: Pam Wheat, Ben Buffington, Tyler Ransdell, Eric Kocher, Ben Klein, Diane Kocher, Bill Sherman, Jeannie Sims, Richie Reigle, Amanda Rosenkrans, Christy Stewart, Cora Best, Lindsey Wasson, Ken Lanik, Linda Mahlia, Pat Mahlia.

KNEELING: Brett Taveau, Phillip Haxel, Joe Skinner, Brooke Renberg, Nabiha Calcuttawala, Jacob Zeiger, Will Sherman, Erin Shadensack.

Puebloans used ladders instead of stairs to go from one floor to another.

CHAPTER 2

GOOPING UP AND SETTING OFF

"Everybody got their hats and sunscreen?" Sara asked. Sara Kelly and Ken Lanik were two Crow Canyon educators guiding the Hannibal kids through their adventure with archaeology. The kids were getting ready to tour the ruins in Woods Canyon, where they'd be excavating later that week.

"Don't forget your water bottles," Sara added. "Newcomers have a hard time remembering how much they need to drink around here. If you get a headache, you're dehydrated. If your muscles start to cramp, you're dehydrated. I don't mean to sound crude, but if you've been out for three hours and don't even sort of have to pee, you'd better drink more water!"

The land around Four Corners doesn't have sand

dunes, but it is like a desert, with plants and trees that can live without much water. Its climate is so dry that sweat evaporates before it can bead up on your skin. It's so dry that by the time you take two pieces of fresh bread and make your sandwich, grab a pickle, some chips, and a drink, the bread already tastes a little stale.

That's not so good for sandwiches. And it's not so good for kids who forget to drink enough water. But it's great for archaeology because a dry climate helps baskets, bones, even buildings last for hundreds of years.

The kids piled into vans and drove past dry grasslands and deep canyons. They saw pinyon pines, cactus, and sagebrush wherever nature chose the landscape, and green fields where farmers watered their crops. If the kids had scratched around one of those sagebrush fields, they might have found a spear point or stone tool. For over a thousand years, ancient Pueblo people had lived all over this land.

"We used to call these people the Anasazi," Ken explained. "But the Navajo gave them that name, which means 'enemy of our people.' So you can understand why their current relatives don't like it. Since we don't know what

Cactus thrives in this hot, dry climate.

Piles of blocks . . .

. . . were once tall towers.

they named themselves, we call them the ancestral Puebloans."

"Try to say 'ancestral Puebloans' three times real fast," muttered one kid who had trouble saying it even once. Generally, the kids tried to say "ancestral Puebloans" instead of "Anasazi," but change takes time. Sometimes they forgot.

"Everybody out for Woods Canyon," said Sara as the vans rolled to a stop. "Grab your water bottles and let's go."

A few minutes down the path, Ben B. stopped and stared at the ground. "I found something," he called out.

"Congratulations," said Sara. "We call these pottery pieces 'potsherds.'"

"'Sherd is nice," said Tyler as he looked at its painted black design.

"You'll see artifacts as you walk along," said Sara. "It's okay to pick something up to look at it, but mark its place with your foot so you can return it to the right spot. Archae-ologists get a lot of information from an item's location."

"Could it really make much difference if you moved it?" asked Ben B.

"Sure. Villages two hundred years apart in age can be built just one hundred feet from each other," answered Ken. "It can be confusing if you put something from a newer settlement into the older one."

"And, don't forget, taking artifacts from public lands like Woods Canyon is against the law," Sara added. "Just think about it this way. You can learn a lot from these artifacts

"Seeing an old brick wall underneath a cliff was the neatest thing. How many times in your life do you get to see anything seven hundred years old still standing?"
NABIHA

because they're still here. If you picked them all up, there wouldn't be any left for your kids or their kids to enjoy."

"Anyway, archaeology is more than finding neat stuff. It's finding out about the people who left all that neat stuff," added Pat Mahlia, the teacher who came with them from Hannibal.

"It *is* tempting," said Christy. "You want to take home a piece of history. Still, it's just not right."

As the kids scrambled into the canyon, Sara pointed to some rocks that used to be a tower. Imagining that pile of rubble as a tall building was hard. In fact, the kids walked

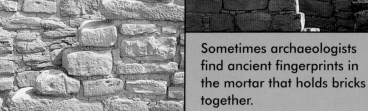

Sometimes archaeologists find ancient fingerprints in the mortar that holds bricks together.

"The amazing thing about this scenery is that it looks professionally done."   NABIHA

"We saw cool stuff like potsherds, Anasazi ruins, cow poop, a deer leg— you know, the usual."   ERIN

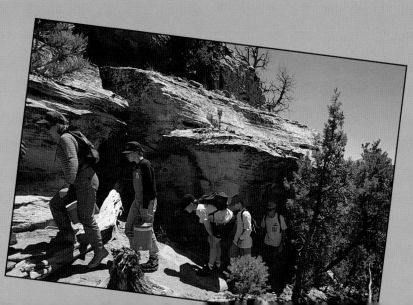

past many mounds and piles without even noticing them. It takes training to see what used to be.

"Look carefully," said Sara as they all gathered on a cliff. "That spot used to be an underground circular room called a kiva. Over there on that cliff is where people built their homes."

"They were excellent builders," Ken added. "They figured out that structures would last longer if they made them wider at the bottom than the top."

The kids took a moment to study the canyon. Some noticed how deep it was. Others listened to the wind. Still others tried to imagine the people living there 750 years ago.

"I thought about how different it must have been for them," said Phillip.

"It's so awesome, so big and open," said Nabiha on the way back to the van. "I wish I could take this home to Hannibal."

Why Did They Leave?

Why did the ancestral Puebloans leave? In the 1200s, many groups built their pueblos, or towns, around springs. Some even put towers near their water supply to guard it. Could a water shortage be the answer?

Trees create new rings of growth each year—wider rings during years with wet weather, narrower ones during dry years. Scientists, looking at thirteenth-century tree rings from this region, discovered a long drought from A.D. 1274 to 1299. Less rain meant less food from crops, less water for drinking, and perhaps less reason to stick around.

Trees can tell stories, sometimes human ones. Archaeologists can find out when a home was built, for example, by looking at its beams. Dendrochronology, or tree-ring dating, is so accurate, scientists can usually tell the exact year a tree died.

An Ancient Pueblo Timeline

Kivas were used for normal living and special religious ceremonies.

As long as ten thousand years ago, people roamed the Four Corners. They gathered wild seeds and cactus fruits and used spears to hunt animals that are now extinct, like the wooly mammoth.

By the year A.D. 1, people in the Four Corners were growing corn and squash and living on the mesa tops in circular houses built with logs and mud. They still hunted, but with bows and arrows. By A.D. 550, they planted beans along with their corn and squash. They stored these foods in baskets and cooked them in clay pots.

As time went on, people clustered their homes together in rows of connected rooms. In front, they built kivas for the village to share. They traded with other groups for red pottery and cotton and shell beads that came from what is now Mexico.

Over the years, villages grew larger. Some had buildings four stories high. Large plazas built on kiva roofs provided a place to work and visit. By A.D. 1150, tens of thousands of people lived in the area.

About 1200, villages moved from mesas to alcoves in the middle of cliffs. These new stone cities had towers and kivas and hundreds of rooms. There, people traded and made beautiful pots and weavings and jewelry.

By 1300, the villages were empty of voices and laughter. The people were gone.

Beans, squash, and especially corn were an essential part of the Puebloan food supply.

CHAPTER 3

THE FACTS ABOUT ARTIFACTS

Before the kids dug them up, they needed to know more about artifacts. The first thing they learned is that an artifact is something made or used by people. A rock in a river most likely isn't an artifact. But it becomes one as soon as it's placed with others in a ring around a fire or shaped into an axe head.

Artifacts tell the story of how people live. "If I was wearing a parka on a hot day like today, you might say I was crazy," said Sara. "But generally, if I wore a heavy jacket, you'd know I lived in a cold place. Clothes tell you a lot about someone's environment."

The kids got a clearer picture of the ancient Pueblo world by looking at the things its people had used. Sometimes just figuring out what an artifact was was hard enough. Phillip wondered if a skull came from a pet dog or a small animal eaten as food. "They're trying to fool us. I bet this is just a rock," Bill joked, as he puzzled over a big stone that turned out to be a corn-grinding tool.

"So far I'm having a terrific time. I kind of don't like that I know I'm learning, it makes it seem more like school."
BEN B.

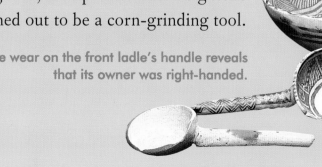

The wear on the front ladle's handle reveals that its owner was right-handed.

17

"This could be a saber-toothed tiger," Erin joked.

Sara pointed out that just labeling an artifact isn't enough. "You'll hear this all week long," she said. "It's not what you find, it's what you find out. Archaeology isn't just finding stuff, it's finding out what it means. A pot can be near some corncobs and the remains of a fire or in a kiva surrounded by turquoise—same pot, but totally different uses that tell us different things."

Sometimes looking at the way an object was damaged provided a clue of how it was used. When Joe realized he was holding a piece of bone, he asked Sara why it was black.

"It's burned," she said. "Why would you burn bone?"

"Sacrifice?" Joe said.

"That's a good guess. Could there be another reason?"

"Food?"

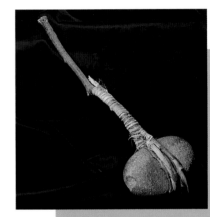

The kids had no problem identifying this stone axe.

Puebloans hunted with stone-tipped spears for hundreds of years.

18

One kid asked if these cooking pots were too wobbly on tables, but ancient Puebloans didn't have tables. These pots were designed for their world. Round bottoms are stronger and more stable when set into sand or fire.

"That's right, cooking," said Sara. "This bone was left over from someone's dinner."

Later Joe looked at the painted design on a piece of pottery. "That's a pitchfork, so we know that they farmed," he concluded.

"Let's think this one out," said Ken. "What do we use pitchforks for?"

"Hay."

"And why do farmers pitch hay?"

"To feed animals."

"Have we seen any bones from cows and horses, the type of animals that eat hay?" asked Ken.

"No," Joe admitted. "Then why did they make a design that looked like a pitchfork?"

"Well, that does look like a pitchfork—to us," said Ken. "One problem archaeologists have is we're looking at another culture with ideas formed by our own. We're influenced by the things we know and the things we believe. We can't be certain these people were thinking the same way."

One kid thought that these sandals woven from the yucca plant looked like "pre-historic Tevas."

Luckily, scientists have another way to learn about the ancient Pueblo world. The people who left the Four Corners in the late 1200s joined up with other Pueblo groups. What some people see as archaeology is family history for many of today's Pueblo tribes. Understanding how current

Pueblo people live can provide a window into the past. By looking at how today's Hopi and Zuni people weave, for example, researchers learned that the loops on kiva walls held looms.

Forgetting pots and hammer stones for a moment, Bill wondered what future scientists would say about the artifacts in his bedroom. "People from seven hundred years ago look so primitive to us," he said. "Future archaeologists might think the same about us. Still, I think they'd be amazed by my stereo."

Sometimes artifacts can be mysterious. The kids thought these things might be (clockwise from the lower left) a hat, a helmet, a shoehorn, an incense burner, and a bedpan. They are really a basket, a broken pot, a scraping tool, an atlatl, and a ladle.

Will future archaeologists wonder whether this frisbee is a toy or a plate? What will they think about these other mysterious artifacts?

Why Did They Leave?

Was a bad drought enough to drive these people away? Maybe. But by looking at even older tree rings, scientists found that ancestral Puebloans had already survived droughts worse than the one in the late 1200s.

As their population grew, the Puebloans had more mouths to feed, more bodies to clothe, more homes to build. In older settlements, archaeologists have found bones from big animals like elk and deer. Bones from later communities show hunters caught smaller animals like rabbits to eat. Could these people have used up the resources around them and needed to move on?

Plants and Animals of the Pueblo World

The juniper's berries flavored food; its wood was used as fuel and as lumber to build homes. Juniper bark soaks up water; that's why mothers used it for baby diapers (the inner bark is softer than you think!).

Sagebrush wood was used as fuel and roofing material. Its leaves were brewed into a tea to treat colds.

Without shopping malls, ancestral Puebloans got what they needed from the natural world. And they used just about every part of the plants and animals around them. A deer, for example, was a little department store, providing flesh for meat, hide for clothing, bones for sewing tools, antlers for scraping and smoothing arrowheads. Puebloans even used deer tendons to tie the arrowheads onto their shafts.

Turkeys were domesticated by the ancient Puebloans.

The pinyon pine's nuts were eaten raw, roasted, and ground into flour. Its wood was used for fuel and building. Pinyon sap, spread onto baskets, made the baskets waterproof.

Ancestral Puebloans ate the yucca's fruit and flowers and pounded its roots into soap. They stripped its leaves into fibers and twisted them into ropes, frayed them into paintbrushes, and wove them into sandals, baskets, and blankets.

The Puebloans used spears and, later, bows and arrows to hunt deer.

Rabbits were chased into giant nets and killed with clubs. They provided meat and fur for winter cloaks and blankets.

CHAPTER 4

DIGGING INTO THE PAST

"**W**e're trying to figure out how many people lived in Woods Canyon and how they related to other people nearby," said Ken. "We need to find artifacts to answer these questions. So your work is really necessary."

The kids were ready to dig. They had studied all kinds of artifacts, from necklaces to cooking pots. They now knew that important clues could be easily overlooked. What first seemed like a regular rock with one smooth side, for example, could really be a grinding stone that had been flattened by crushing corn.

"The first time I filled my bucket, I found nothing. But when I sifted, I found one big potsherd I could have kicked myself for not having seen, two really small potsherds, and a small piece of adobe."

JACOB

Back in the lab, the kids had also learned how to dig—archaeologist style. They had marked off an area and carefully used trowels to skim off thin layers of dirt. This dirt went into buckets to be screened or sifted for tiny treasures like nuggets of charcoal and pottery beads. If the kids had found a larger artifact, they removed all the dirt around it first. Once they saw that nothing else was nearby, they could pick it up.

After all this practice, the kids felt excited about finding potsherds and arrowheads. But, as they walked down the path to Woods Canyon, they were a little nervous about finding other things.

"What if we find human remains?" Jeannie asked.

"I think I'd die myself," said Amanda.

Sara explained Crow Canyon's policy: If you start to uncover human bones, call the archaeologist, who will cover them back up. "It's a dilemma," she said. "If you don't analyze human bones, you lose information about what people ate and how they worked and died.

"But if you do," she continued, "you're being disrespectful to Native Americans. And there has been a lot of disrespect in the past. Back East, for instance, archaeologists once dug up two graves. They thought one skeleton was a white

"You could look on the ground and see potsherds all over." JOE

"When in doubt, don't throw it out. Put it in your artifact bag," an archaeologist said. "We'd rather discard something in the lab than miss out on an artifact."

person and the other a Native American. They brought out a priest to bless the Anglo bones and rebury them. They put the Native American bones in a museum."

"How would you feel if someone just went into the cemetery and dug up the bones of someone you once knew?" said Will. "I'd be pretty angry."

In the canyon, the kids split into three groups and followed different archaeologists to test pits around the site. In archaeologist Mark Varien's group, one boy said he had thought the whole village would be excavated. Mark explained that just uncovering small sections leaves untouched areas for future scientists to make new discoveries with better technology.

"This is harder than I expected," Tyler said, scraping at dirt that had been packed down for seven hundred years.

"It is hard," said Ben K. "It's worth it though. I found a potsherd and a fragment of animal bone."

"What if I find something great, but it's on the ground and not in my pit?" Brett asked.

"Leave it, unless it's something fantastic like a piece of ancient wood big enough to use in dating the site," said Mark. "I always say things look prettier out here than in a box in a museum."

Measuring exactly where you find an artifact helps date it. Normally, the deeper you go in a pit, the older the artifacts. (Imagine the dates on a pile of magazines you stack up month by month.)

Once work at Woods Canyon was completed, archaeologists used this screened dirt to fill in the test pits. Some kids hated the idea of covering up their work, but it protects sites from weather and theft.

Meanwhile, in archaeologist Melissa Churchill's area, kids were digging in a midden, or trash heap. Ancient garbage is an archaeologist's treasure chest. Think of how much someone could learn about your life from the pizza box, ripped jeans, and old telephone bill in your trash can. Broken pottery and tools and worn-out clothing help archaeologists learn about daily life in ancient times.

In the space of a morning, the kids had dug into the Stone Age.

"Watch out, coming through," said Melissa, who was helping Jeannie shake her bucket of dirt through the large screen at their digging site.

"I see something greenish," Melissa said. "Can you find it?"

"It's a flake," said Nabiha, picking up the chip of rock left over when someone made a stone tool.

"I haven't found anything yet," said Brooke.

"Remember, it's not what you find, it's what you find out," said Jeannie.

"Yeah," Brooke answered. "But it's fun to find stuff."

In archaeologist Jeff Blomster's section, Eric and Jacob were digging down to a roof that had collapsed into its kiva.

"I'm starting to hit adobe," called Eric, as he picked up a reddish-brown lump the size of a marble.

"Yes, you've got adobe," said Jeff. "They plastered their roofs with it."

A moment later, Eric called out again. "I found a piece of corrugated pottery right here."

"If you find more in that spot, let me know and we'll put it on the map," Jeff said. "It could mean they're all part of the same vessel. If so, we might put it back together in the lab."

At the end of the day, the kids wrote down exactly how far they'd dug and what they had found.

After two sweaty days of digging, the kids had different feelings about the care and patience needed to do archaeology.

"I don't think I'd like to be an archaeologist—at least not in Colorado," said Lindsey. "It's too hot."

"It's fun for a week," said Ben B. "But it's too boring to do my whole life."

"I don't know," said Erin, "it's neat finding things that people didn't leave for you."

"Digging in the unit made me feel like I was actually an archaeologist," Will said. "It was kind of like a good book where you feel involved."

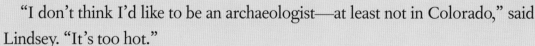

Why Did They Leave?

Did ancestral Puebloans move because they ran out of resources? Maybe. But archaeologists do think they were able to grow enough corn to feed themselves.

Could fear have been the answer? Moving into cliff dwellings made a lot of sense if these people were trying to protect themselves. Their homes couldn't be seen from the mesas above. They were hard to attack. Archaeologists have found evidence suggesting some people during this time period died violently. Did the ancestral Puebloans move because they were afraid their families were in danger?

THE SCIENTIFIC PROCESS

When they want to learn about past cultures, archaeologists don't just grab a shovel. Every scientific project begins with a specific set of questions to be answered. Since drought was a reason ancestral Puebloans might have moved, one question Crow Canyon archaeologists are asking is how Woods Canyon residents used their water supply. In fact, archaeologists decided to dig at Woods Canyon because they saw the ruins of a water reservoir.

The next step in the scientific process is to accurately record an experiment. When archaeologists excavate a site, they list exactly what artifacts they find and where they find them. These descriptions let future archaeologists use the information in their work.

Once an experiment is finished, scientists must analyze the information they found. In archaeol-

Chris Pierce is studying cooking pots to understand why ancestral Puebloans changed from using smooth pots to ones with ridges.

ology, a lot of this analysis happens in the laboratory, where artifacts reveal even more secrets about the past. With a microscope, for example, scientists can see how a tool is worn. These patterns can tell them if a stone axe was used as a weapon or for cutting sagebrush. Testing the insides of pots can show what was cooked in them.

When she heard that the last step in the process is bringing all this information into a report, Nabiha asked, "Can't you hire someone else to do it?" But part of an archaeologist's job is describing a dig and how it answered research questions. This report lets other scientists compare how people lived at Woods Canyon, for example, with life in other communities. Careful storage of the artifacts allows future archaeologists to come back to them with new questions.

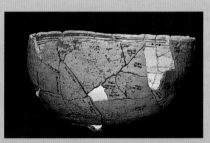

Why potters used certain designs is a mystery. "You can find out what people were doing by the things they left behind," said Sara. "Finding out what they were thinking is much harder."

Archaeologists in the early 1900s didn't know about tree-ring dating, so they used roof beams for firewood. Even though they didn't do it on purpose, they lost very important information. This mug is being stored in plastic for the future scientists who might have better ways to examine it.

CHAPTER 5

TRYING OUT THE OLD WAYS

Digging up artifacts isn't the only way archaeologists learn about the past. Learning about past cultures includes knowing how they did things. That's why archaeologists at Crow Canyon built a pithouse, the type of home the ancestral Puebloans made around A.D. 700. Kids helped the archaeologists make their pithouse by using ancient building techniques. After a lot of tired muscles and sore backs, they had even more reason to appreciate prehistoric people.

"Imagine using a stick and a basket to remove three feet of dirt," said Sara to the kids as they sat inside the pithouse. "Think about cutting down all the trees you'd need to build this thing. It takes about an hour just to cut through an inch of trunk with a stone axe.

"And it took several truckloads of willow to weave between beams to make the walls," she continued. "That's a lot of armloads when you don't have a pickup."

"I could live in this," said Brett. "It's cool."

In a pithouse, a whole family lived in one room, sleeping on yucca mats with woven feather blankets. As food was cooked in a fire pit, smoke went out a hole in the roof.

Testing old methods provides many insights about how and why things were done. Archaeologists used to think, for example, that ancient people burned the tops of wooden beams to cut them. Once they tried it themselves, scientists realized that charred beams keep out termites.

The fancy name for trying out ancient ways is *experimental archaeology*. Doing a little experimental archaeology themselves, the kids performed some daily chores of the ancient Pueblo world.

"It made me realize how hard they worked," said Erin.

And it made other kids realize how hard the work was. "All I'd be good for," joked Jeannie, "would be to kill for extra food!"

GRINDING CORN

Talk about Stone Age. Women used manos, hand-sized stones, to grind dried corn on metates, stone slabs. Eventually the flour was cooked into flat breads or mush. Unfortunately, these foods had an added ingredient. Tiny bits of stone broke off and mixed in with the corn. After years of chewing this food, many people's teeth were ground to stubs.

"It's harder than I thought to get it small," said Ben K. after he tried grinding his share of corn.

"I was surprised to find there was really a pattern to using a mano and metate," said Jacob. "I ate some—bland, but not half bad."

Lindsey disagreed. "It looks like school chalk," she said, "and it tastes like school chalk."

STARTING FIRES

Start by making a nest of shredded juniper bark or cattail fluff. Twirl a stick on a little board until friction heats things up. Poof, you've got fire.

"Sara made it look easy," said Joe, "but when me and Phillip tried to start one, we couldn't even get smoke."

"I would've killed for a box of matches," added Jacob.

MAKING POTTERY

Sara demonstrated how ancient Puebloans formed coils of clay into a bowl. Then she used a piece of gourd to scrape them smooth. The kids started making their own pots and bowls and ladles.

"My pot sorta looks like Mr. Potato Head without eyes or a mouth," said Erin. "But I think the Anasazi would be impressed if they saw us trying to learn their ways."

"I bet they didn't use a knife to cut the tops of their mugs," said Brooke, as she reached for one herself.

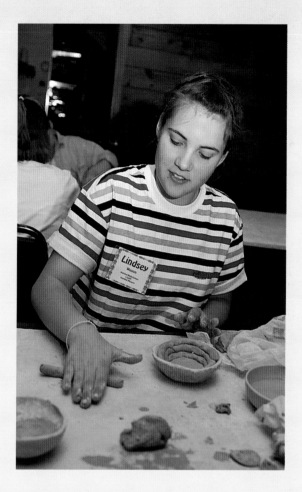

"They certainly didn't use steel ones," answered Sara, "but they had blades made from obsidian that were even sharper. Sometimes we're so proud of our own technology, we are blind to how advanced ancient cultures actually were."

Bill learned to appreciate a potter's skill when he tried to paint a traditional design on his pot with a brush made from yucca leaves. "Oops," he said as he made a mistake. "I guess I'll make a stripe instead."

"We should bury these pots and see what archaeologists think when they find them," said Joe.

"They're gonna think there were some lame Anasazis," Jacob answered.

HUNTING

Before they developed the bow and arrow, Pueblo hunters used the atlatl. This flat stick helped launch spears faster than throwing them freehand. When prehistoric men used atlatls and stone-tipped spears, they brought down deer and elk. The kids tried to hit a plastic turkey.

"They're easy to throw," commented Richie after his turn with the atlatl. "It's just hard to hit the turkey."

"I think we'd be eating corn for dinner," said Cora.

PLAYING GAMES

"In modern times, Pueblo kids have played these games and we think their ancestors might have played them too," said Ken. "I like teaching them to you. When we just focus on what ancestral

Puebloans ate and built, it's easy to forget that they were people who laughed and played games."

Ken showed the kids how to play Hoop and Stick, a relay race where each team member uses a stick to toss a hoop of willow branches the length of the field and back. Then the kids formed a circle to play the Rattle Game. In this game, a blindfolded person tries to tag someone who is darting around while shaking a rattle made from a gourd and beans. The game might have taught ancient children listening skills that helped them hunt. The kids from Hannibal just thought it was fun.

They played until lunch but still weren't ready to quit. "Can we play this some more?" asked Ben B. "It's an important cultural experience."

Why Did They Leave?

Did the ancestral Puebloans move because of fear? Maybe. But who were they afraid of? Archaeologists know that villages had a history of trading with each other, so we can't be sure they were afraid of their neighbors. And the earliest archaeological evidence of other groups coming into the area doesn't begin for another hundred years.

Maybe ancestral Puebloans weren't being pushed out of their old home, but were pulled toward something new. In the south, other groups practiced a religion that helped bring their communities together. Since ancestral Puebloans did move south, they may have been attracted by a religion that helped them live more peacefully.

Kachinas are dolls like this one. But, to the Pueblo people, kachinas are also spirits who bring, among other things, rain and blessings. Some archaeologists think it was belief in these spirits that helped draw people away from the Four Corners.

Modern Hopi believe this petroglyph symbol is a kachina who helped inspire the Puebloans' travels.

CHAPTER 6

UISITING THE PAST

"I find myself looking for potsherds everywhere," said Brett, "even in this parking lot."

Brett's parking lot was at Mesa Verde National Park where the kids were spending the last day of their trip. Mesa Verde is a park created to preserve the works of prehistoric people. The location was a good choice. Mesa Verde has over four thousand archaeological sites, including six hundred cliff dwellings.

Visiting Mesa Verde was a perfect ending to the kids' week at Crow Canyon. It summed up much of what they learned about ancestral Puebloans. Fully excavated ruins helped them more clearly picture how villages were laid out. And after a week of study, they could look at a ruin and say, "There's the kiva." Or, "These rooms were used for storage."

Mesa Verde was like a time machine where the kids could visit a pithouse built in A.D. 500, a rectangular village from A.D. 950, and finally, thirteenth-century cliff

"Today was my favorite event of our Colorado trip. I think I liked it because I got to see actual sites that were fully excavated." JOE

Built starting around A.D. **1190, Balcony House was home to about forty people.**

dwellings. Moving from one to the other, the kids could see how society—and people's individual lives—changed over time.

"As they got more experience, they got smarter," said Bill. "You can see how they made their houses better through the years."

"I think the ones in later years had it easier," said Amanda. "The earlier ones had to come up with all the ideas that the later people could improve on."

It was those "later people" who built the last ruin on the kids' schedule. With only thirty-five rooms, Balcony House wasn't the park's largest cliff dwelling, but it was one of the most exciting. Tucked under an overhanging cliff and six hundred feet above the canyon floor, Balcony House was a great example of how ancient Puebloans kept defense in mind when they built their final homes in this region. Back then, people could only enter Balcony House through a long tunnel carved into the rock. A hand-and-toe-hold trail led to the mesa top above. Whether they were afraid of others or not, the residents of Balcony House made it very hard to get in and out of their home.

The kids got in thanks to modern ladders and railings. To some, that seemed hard enough.

"It's definitely not a place for someone who is afraid of heights," said Will.

"I'm not nervous of heights," Lindsey replied, "just of falling off heights."

But every kid agreed the climb was worth it. They admired the wall that kept them and ancient Puebloans from falling over the steep cliff. They peeked into rooms and thought of sleeping on beds of juniper bark and animal

"I felt like a rock climber." AMANDA

skins. They looked at kiva walls blackened by smoke and imagined spending cold winters by a fire.

"I really enjoyed climbing those steep ladders even though I'm terrified of high places. I thought I was going to die when you had to scale that cliff by placing your feet in footholes." CORA

"This house may not look like your house, but these people were like us," said Dawn O'Sickey, the park ranger who led their tour. "No, they didn't have computers or vans. Yes, they spent long days planting and finding their food. But they also found time to do things they enjoyed. They didn't need paint on their pottery for it to hold water. They didn't wear necklaces to keep themselves warm in winter.

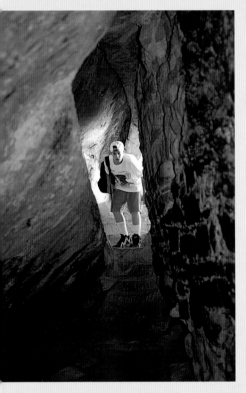

Built later than the actual village, this tunnel really helps Balcony House's defense. You can't get ready to throw a spear when you're crawling through a tunnel.

"These buildings aren't just stone," Dawn continued. "They were people's homes. Babies cried here. Two-year-olds broke their parents' best pots. Older children whined, 'Do I have to grind the corn now?' Young men and women were drawn to each other and made families. And became grandparents who passed stories on to new children.

"These people lived their lives with what they had and tried to do better—just like people today. We may never understand exactly why they built T-shaped doorways or why they left this area. But since we understand what it

The kids went down into a kiva at Spruce Tree House. "I was surprised how much light there was in it from a little opening in the roof," said Ben B.

means to be human, we know the most important thing about them."

Thinking over his week, Bill agreed with Dawn. "My favorite part is that you realize that the Anasazi were human beings, not just things that are dead and gone."

"I have realized how important every little artifact is," said Jeannie. "Each artifact can tell or complete a story. Before this week, I probably could have cared less who bothered what [artifact], but now I do."

"This was a good experience," said Christy. "I was glad I could help aid science. I think being an archaeologist would be a fun job."

"I thought it was going to be just like a bunch of school days strung together," said Jeannie, "but I want to come back."

Why people built these T-shaped doorways is a mystery. Some archaeologists think they were designed to be covered with a rock slab to block out cold but still provide ventilation. "I thought they might have that so the Anasazis could carry things like pots or baskets on their heads," said Richie.

The kids were especially respectful at Spruce Tree House because some Pueblo people consider it to be their spiritual home.

Why Did They Leave?

Which theory about why ancestral Puebloans left the Four Corners is right? Maybe they all are. Maybe none of these reasons were quite enough to convince them to leave, but all of them put together. . . .

What if the population had been growing for years, using up local resources? And what if drought meant there were not only fewer natural resources but fewer crops as well? And what if this shortage of food and water created tension between neighbors? And what if people, under all this stress, heard about a better, easier life in the south?

The dig at Woods Canyon should help supply some answers. Analyzing where the clay in its pottery actually came from will tell archaeologists if different villages associated with each other. Looking at the reservoir will help explain how people coped with drought. Gaining an understanding of life in this village and other ones will help scientists see the bigger picture.

We may never know exactly why these ancient Puebloans left their home-land but, after their week at Crow Canyon, the kids had their own ideas. "I like the theory about how their food was getting used up," said Bill. "We see that today, people moving someplace better when they run out of resources."

"I don't know," said Amanda, "I think it's still a big mystery."

"I wouldn't have left if I were them," said Jacob. "I like it here a lot."

Home to some Pueblo people
seven hundred years ago . . .

BILL BONEBRAKE

. . . and home to some Pueblo
people today. This is the Taos
Pueblo in New Mexico.

Glossary

ADOBE—sun-dried clay

ANCESTRAL PUEBLOANS—people, also known as the Anasazi, who lived in the Four Corners area of the American Southwest from about A.D. 1 to about A.D. 1200

ANGLO—a slang name for an English-speaking, white North American

ARCHAEOLOGY—the science that studies past cultures by looking at the things they left behind

ARTIFACTS—things made or used by people in their daily lives

ATLATL—a spear-throwing device used by many ancient peoples

CORRUGATED POTTERY—pottery with surface indentations that ancestral Puebloans used for cooking

DEHYDRATED—to have lost water and become dry

DENDROCHRONOLOGY—dating wood by comparing its tree rings with samples of known age

DROUGHT—a long period with no rain

EXCAVATION—uncovering objects from the past by the carefully planned digging of a site

KIVA—a round underground room used for cooking, eating, sleeping, and religious ceremonies

MANO—a hand-held stone used to grind corn

MESA—land that has a flat top and steep sides

METATE—a flat stone slab used in grinding corn

MIDDEN—a trash heap

OBSIDIAN—black hard glass formed from volcanic lava

PETROGLYPH—a picture carved into rock

POTSHERD—a broken piece of pottery

RESERVOIR—a natural or artificial pond used to store water

SCREEN—to sift dirt to look for small artifacts

TREE-RING DATING— *see* DENDROCHRONOLOGY

When Eric learned that ancestral Puebloan men only averaged five feet, four inches, he said, "I would have been abnormal!"

Further Reading

OTHER BOOKS ABOUT THE ANCIENT AND CURRENT PUEBLO PEOPLE

Ancona, George. *Earth Daughter: Alicia of Acoma Pueblo*. New York: Simon & Schuster, 1995.

Arnold, Caroline. *The Ancient Cliff Dwellers of Mesa Verde*. New York: Clarion Books, 1992.

Fisher, Leonard Everett. *Anasazi*. New York: Atheneum, 1997.

Keegan, Marcia. *Pueblo Boy: Growing up in Two Worlds*. New York: Cobblehill Books, 1991.

Warren, Scott. *Cities in the Sand: The Ancient Civilizations of the Southwest*. San Francisco: Chronicle Books, 1992.

OTHER BOOKS ABOUT ARCHAEOLOGY

Hackwell, W. John. *Digging to the Past: Excavations in Ancient Lands*. New York: Charles Scribner's Sons, 1986.

James, Carollyn. *Digging Up the Past: The Story of an Archaeological Adventure*. New York: Franklin Watts, 1990.

Porell, Bruce. *Digging the Past: Archaeology in Your Own Backyard*. Reading, MA: Addison Wesley, 1979.

FOR MORE INFORMATION, CONTACT:

Crow Canyon Archaeological Center

23390 County Road K

Cortez, Colorado 81321

Tel: 1-800-422-8975

Web page: www@crowcanyon.org